C152053825

# Awesome Bugs

# BEETLES
and
other BUGS

Anna Claybourne

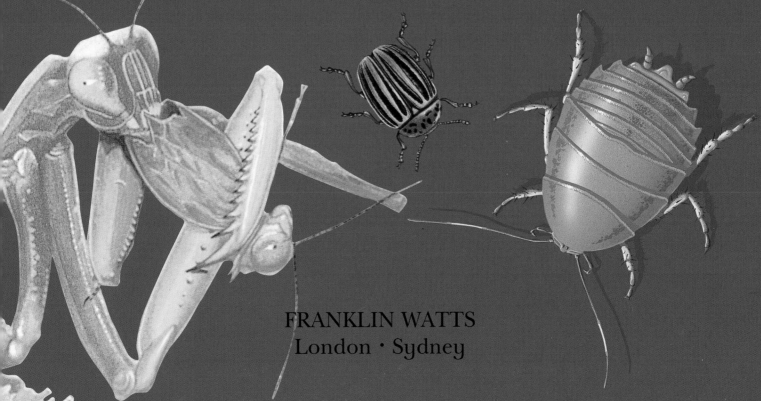

FRANKLIN WATTS
London · Sydney

© Aladdin Books Ltd 2003

*Produced by:*
Aladdin Books Ltd
28 Percy Street
London W1P 2BZ

ISBN 0–7496–4946–1

*First published in*
*Great Britain in 2003 by:*
Franklin Watts
96 Leonard Street
London
EC2A 4XD

*Editor:*
Harriet Brown

*Designer:*
Flick, Book Design & Graphics

*Illustrators:*
Norman Barber, Peter Barrett,
Sergio Borella, Dave Burroughs,
Robin Carter, Roy Coombs, Cecilia
Fitzsimons, Elsa Godfrey, Gary
Hincks, Jonathan Latimer, Donald
Myall, Nina O'Connel, Richard
Orr, Alex Pang, John Rignall, Steve
Roberts – Wildlife Art, Rob Shone,
Tony Swift, Myke Taylor, Phillip
Weare, Norman Weaver
*Cartoons:* Jo Moore

Certain illustrations have
appeared in earlier books
created by Aladdin Books.

# Contents

# Introduction

In this book you can find out all about beetles, bugs, flies, fleas, cockroaches and other creepy-crawly insects. Although they're small, insects are mighty. They have lived on the Earth for much longer than humans, and there are millions more of them than there are of us! This book shows where some of these bugs live, and how they find food, grow, breed and defend themselves. You will find giant beetles, killer bugs and insects that look like twigs, leaves and flowers – even insects that live in your kitchen, in your bed or on you!

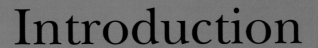

Spot and count, and more fun facts!

**?** Q: Why watch out for these boxes?

A: They give answers to the bug questions you always wanted to ask.

zoom in on...

Bits and pieces
Look out for these boxes to take a closer look at beetle and bug features.

Awesome facts
Watch out for these diamonds to learn more about truly weird and wonderful beetles and other bugs.

**SHIELD BUG**

# What is an insect?

Insects are small, creepy-crawly creatures with six legs. They have three body sections, and two feelers, or antennae. They don't have a skeleton. An insect's body is held together by its tough outer skin, called the exoskeleton.

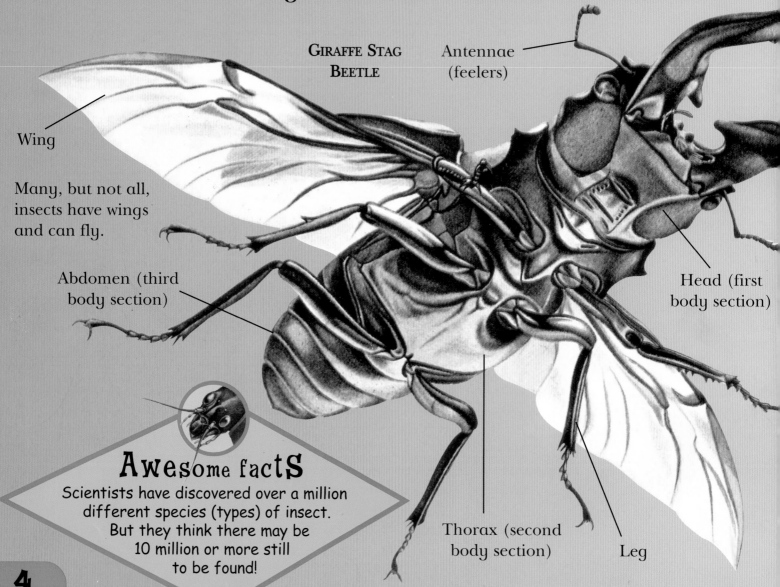

**GIRAFFE STAG BEETLE**

Antennae (feelers)

Wing

Many, but not all, insects have wings and can fly.

Abdomen (third body section)

Head (first body section)

Thorax (second body section)

Leg

## Awesome facts

Scientists have discovered over a million different species (types) of insect. But they think there may be 10 million or more still to be found!

Insects are found all over the world. They live in forests, fields, deserts, rivers, underground, in our houses and on other animals. They all belong to the same family but come in many different shapes and sizes, and are designed for a variety of foods and lifestyles. Some nibble plants, some hunt other animals, some feed on dead bodies and some suck blood. Some even eat carpets, clothes or books!

FLY

GRASSHOPPER

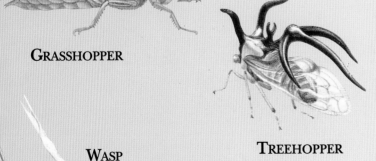

TREEHOPPER

WASP

FLEA

Q: How long have insects been around?

A: Insects first developed between 300 and 400 million years ago. That's long before humans, or even dinosaurs. Fossils show that some insects, like earwigs, have looked the same for millions of years. Others, like dragonflies, used to be much bigger than they are now – up to 1m across!

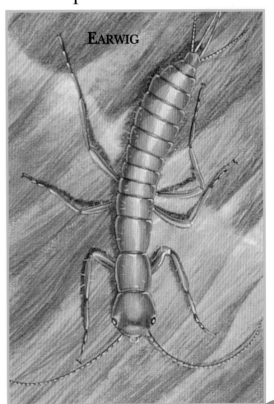

EARWIG

**Q:** Why are so many beetles colourful?

**A:** In the animal world, bright colours often act as a warning to predators (hunters) that an animal tastes bad or is poisonous. This is true for some beetles. Others, like the wasp beetle, mimic (copy) a stinging insect to stay safe.

The tropical flower beetle is from Africa. It feeds on flower nectar and tree sap, so it doesn't need its sharp horns for hunting. Only the males have horns, which may be used for fighting each other. The beetle's wing cases are so beautiful that some people collect them to use as jewels.

**TROPICAL FLOWER BEETLE**

**STAG BEETLE**
Stag beetles get their name from the male's antler-shaped horns.

**Awesome factS**
The goliath beetle from West Africa is the world's biggest beetle. It can grow up to 12 cm long and weighs up to 100 g.

6

# Brilliant beetles

There are more beetles than any other kind of insect. All beetles have biting jaws and hard wing cases called elytra. This gives them a shiny shell, which is often brightly coloured.

**WEEVIL**
Weevils are beetles. They have jaws at the end of their long snout.

**LEAF BEETLE**
This beautiful beetle lives in Asia and Australia. Its strong back legs are used for jumping around, so it is sometimes called the kangaroo beetle. Like many beetles, it feeds on flowers and leaves, often causing damage to crops.

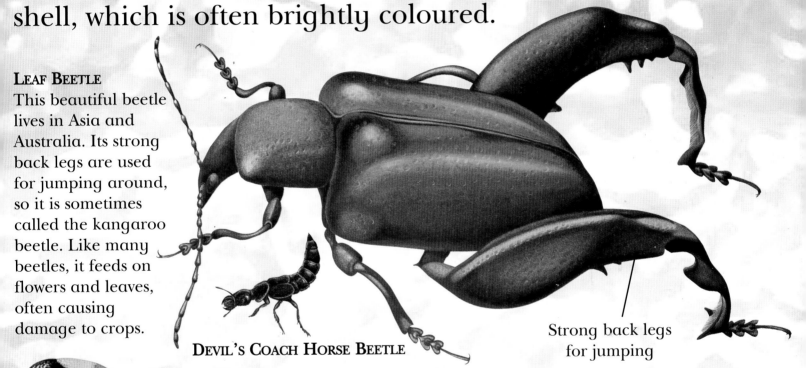

**DEVIL'S COACH HORSE BEETLE**

Strong back legs for jumping

## Flight
In order to fly, a beetle has to lift its elytra high up above its back, so that its wings can open out and move freely. Some beetles, such as the armoured stink beetle, cannot fly because their elytra are joined together.

zoom in on...

7

# True bugs

People use the word 'bugs' to mean any kind of creepy-crawly – but in the insect world, a true bug is a kind of insect. True bugs look a bit like beetles, but instead of jaws they have a sucking mouth shaped like a straw.

HADRODEMUS BUG

Scientists have discovered around 50,000 species of true bugs altogether.

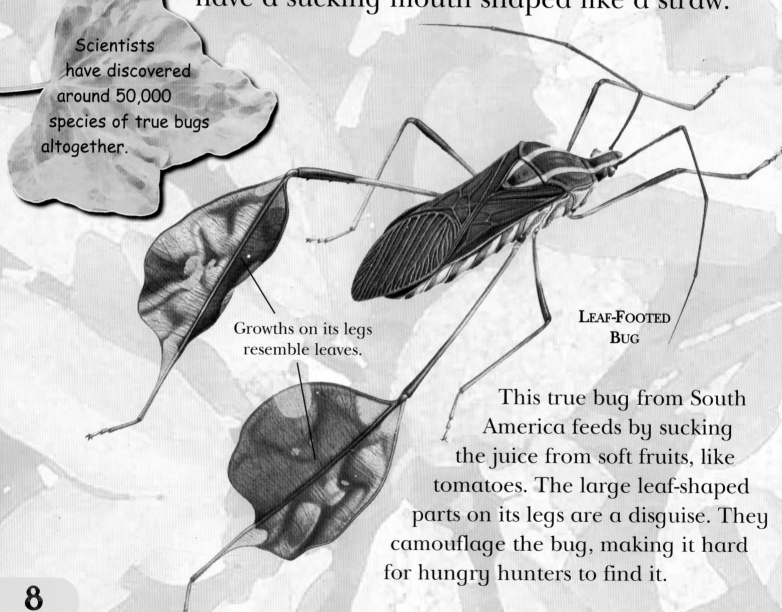

Growths on its legs resemble leaves.

LEAF-FOOTED BUG

This true bug from South America feeds by sucking the juice from soft fruits, like tomatoes. The large leaf-shaped parts on its legs are a disguise. They camouflage the bug, making it hard for hungry hunters to find it.

of rotting flesh if they get squashed.

 Q: Why are treehoppers such strange shapes?

A: Treehoppers are small true bugs that feed on trees. The front parts of some treehoppers' bodies have horns, spikes, hollow lantern shapes or long tubes on them. Scientists think that these shapes may act as camouflage or scare enemies away.

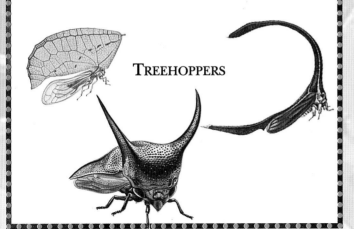

TREEHOPPERS

## Sucking mouths

True bugs use their straw-like, sucking mouthparts to suck up liquid food, such as tree sap, fruit juice or animal blood. A bug's mouth is sometimes called its 'beak'. The beak is often sharp at the tip, so that the bug can pierce its way through plant stems or skin. When it is not feeding, a bug can tuck its beak under its body.

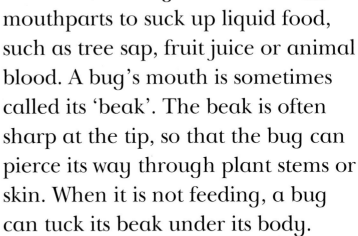

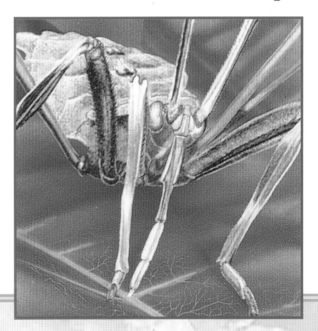

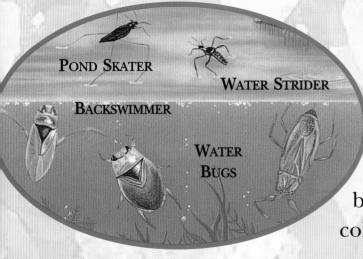

POND SKATER

WATER STRIDER

BACKSWIMMER

WATER BUGS

Many types of true bugs live in rivers and ponds. Some, like pond skaters, balance on the surface of the water and catch insects. Others, like the backswimmer, swim underwater, but collect air from the surface to breathe.

zoom in on...

# Mating and courtship

Most bugs have to get together in pairs of one male and one female, to mate and have babies. There are so many different types of bug, that each one needs a way of tracking down a mate of the same species as itself.

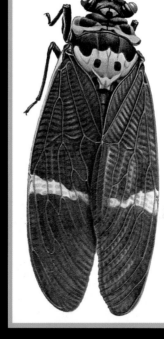

**DEATH'S HEAD CICADA**

Male cicadas attract a mate by vibrating drum-like areas on their sides. This makes a very loud noise that can be heard nearly a kilometre away.

**GLOW-WORM (MALE)**

**GLOW-WORM (FEMALE)**

Glow-worms use patterns of flashes to find their own species in the dark. Males fly about, whilst females sit on a leaf or twig and glow in response.

Q: How does a glow-worm glow?

A: Glow-worms are not worms, but a type of beetle. The tip of a glow-worm's abdomen contains special cells that create a yellow–green light, by combining different chemicals. The glow from a glow-worm is known as 'cold light' because it produces almost no heat.

Female praying mantises (below) are famous for eating the male after mating. In fact, this only happens sometimes if the female is hungry. After mating, the female lays her eggs and also dies.

**EARWIGS**

Male and female earwigs (above) use their antennae to smell and recognise each other when they meet.

## Awesome facts

Male diopsid flies have eyes on long stalks. They compete for females by comparing the length of their eye-stalks. The male with the longest stalks wins!

FEMALE PRAYING
MANTIS

# Eggs and young

A female bug usually lays her eggs from the tip of her abdomen. This ladybird is laying hers on a leaf.

Most beetles and bugs have babies by laying eggs. After laying the eggs, they usually fly away or even die before the babies hatch out. The babies often don't look like their parents at all. They may change several times before becoming adults. This change is called 'metamorphosis'.

**Awesome facts**

Aphids are very unusual because they can have babies without mating or laying eggs! They give birth to live babies that can walk and feed straight away (right).

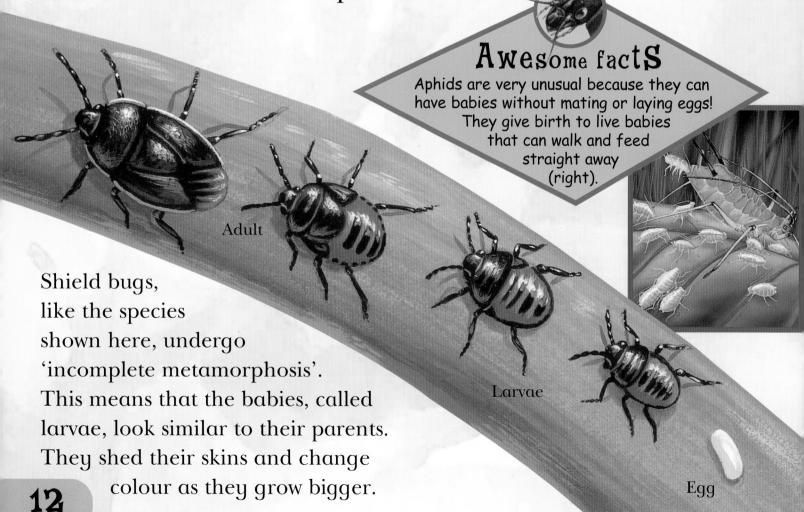

Adult

Larvae

Egg

Shield bugs, like the species shown here, undergo 'incomplete metamorphosis'. This means that the babies, called larvae, look similar to their parents. They shed their skins and change colour as they grow bigger.

**12**

Fungus beetles are unusual in the insect world, because they guard their eggs and care for their babies when they hatch. The babies, or larvae, look like stripy caterpillars. The mother takes them with her to feed on fungus. She rounds them up in a group to keep them safe.

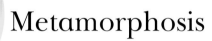

zoom in on...

## Metamorphosis

In some bug species, the babies look completely unlike their parents and live very different lifestyles. For example, dragonfly babies, called nymphs, live underwater. They have no wings, and catch prey using a large hinged jaw that can reach out like a robot arm. After a few years, the nymph climbs out of the water onto a plant stalk. It sheds its skin and emerges as an adult dragonfly with a long tail and wings.

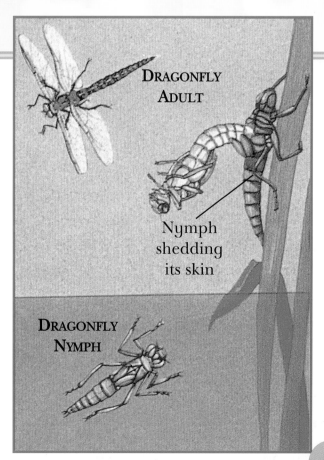

DRAGONFLY ADULT

Nymph shedding its skin

DRAGONFLY NYMPH

A dragonfly can catch and eat its own weight in other insects in less than an hour.

Antlions are the larvae of a type of bug. They catch prey, such as ants, by setting a trap. The antlion digs a round pit in the sandy soil, and waits at the bottom, half-buried in the ground. If an ant comes too close, it tumbles down into the bottom of the pit, where the antlion grabs it using its pincer-shaped jaws.

## zoom in on...

## Killer poison

Some hunting insects, especially true bugs, can only eat liquid food. So they inject their prey with poison that dissolves its insides. The bug can then suck out the juice! This assassin bug is using its long, sharp beak to inject poison into a fly.

(1) The antlion digs the pit by moving around and around in a circle.

(2) When an ant falls in, the antlion grabs it and sucks out its insides.

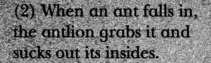

(3) If an ant tries to escape, the antlion throws sand at it to make it fall back down again.

14

# Bug attack!

Although they're small, many bugs are fierce hunters. They kill and eat other insects, spiders, worms, and sometimes creatures such as fish and frogs. They use stings, poisonous bites, sharp jaws or surprise attacks to help them catch and kill their prey.

**GIANT WATER BUG**
This big bug is stabbing a frog with its sharp beak.

Diving beetles live in ponds and lakes, and can grow up to 4 cm long. They are so fierce and deadly that if there's one in your pond, it will wipe out almost all the other wildlife there. They catch prey with their front legs and tear it to pieces with their powerful jaws.

**DIVING BEETLES**

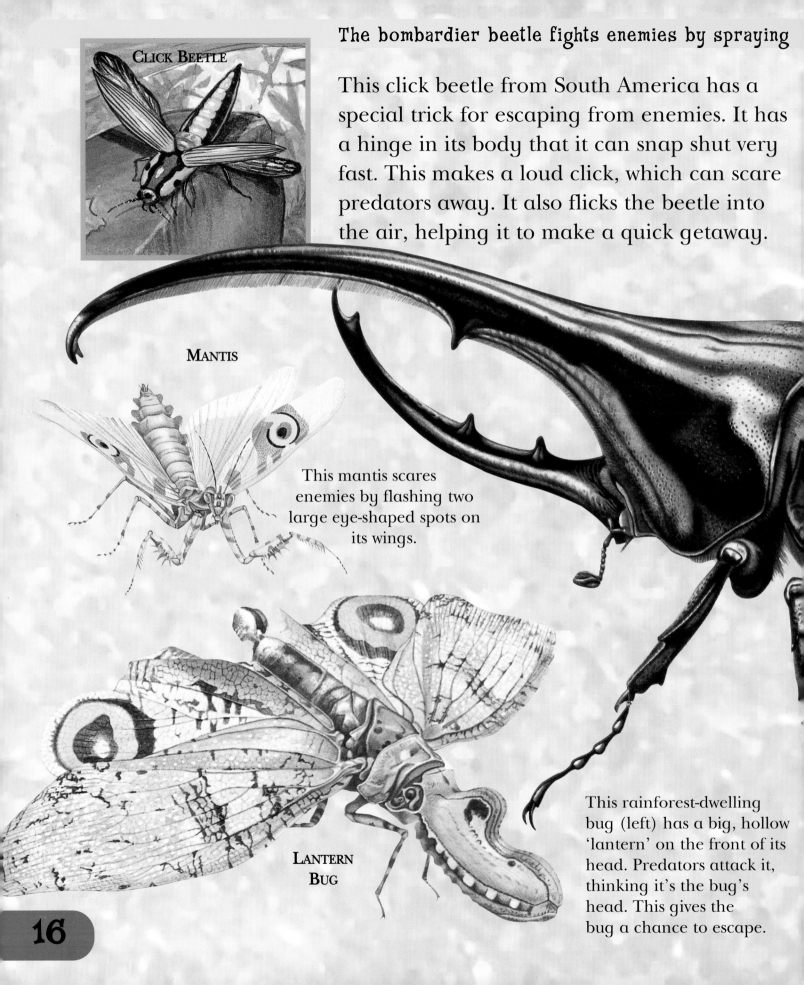

CLICK BEETLE

This click beetle from South America has a special trick for escaping from enemies. It has a hinge in its body that it can snap shut very fast. This makes a loud click, which can scare predators away. It also flicks the beetle into the air, helping it to make a quick getaway.

MANTIS

This mantis scares enemies by flashing two large eye-shaped spots on its wings.

LANTERN BUG

This rainforest-dwelling bug (left) has a big, hollow 'lantern' on the front of its head. Predators attack it, thinking it's the bug's head. This gives the bug a chance to escape.

16

# Staying safe

You might not fancy a bug for lunch, but they make a delicious, protein-packed meal for many animals. Birds, lizards, spiders and other insects all hunt and eat them. So bugs need ways to hide and to fight off enemies.

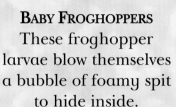

**BABY FROGHOPPERS**
These froghopper larvae blow themselves a bubble of foamy spit to hide inside.

*zoom in on...*

## Chemical sprays

Many insects squirt or spray nasty chemicals at their attackers. The bombardier beetle releases hot, poisonous gas from a special chamber at the tip of its abdomen. It's enough to scare away a frog or lizard.

**HERCULES BEETLE**

This scary-looking beetle is one of the biggest insects in the world. Its long horns may frighten away some predators. But if that doesn't work, the Hercules beetle can squirt a smelly brown liquid from its abdomen which puts off most attackers.

**BOMBARDIER BEETLE**

17

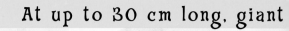
# Bug disguises

Many bugs are brilliant at camouflage –
disguising themselves so that they are
hard to see. Some have patterns and
shapes that match their surroundings.
Others imitate something that tastes
bad, to keep predators away.

**Q: Is camouflage always used to hide from hunters?**

A: Not at all. Hunting bugs
use camouflage too – to hide
from their prey! The pink
flower mantis hides on a pink
flower, then leaps out to grab
other insects that fly past.

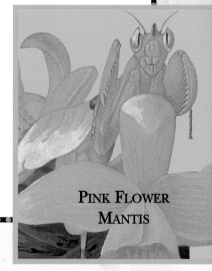

PINK FLOWER
MANTIS

THORN BUGS

The thorn bug's whole body is shaped like a hard,
spiky thorn. This protects it in two ways. Firstly,
when it sits still, it can pretend to be part of a
plant. Secondly, if a predator does try to eat it,
the hard spikes will hurt the predator's mouth.

COMMON
STICK
INSECT

Stick insects and leaf insects get their names because they look just like parts of a plant. When they sit still on a plant, it can be almost impossible to find them. Some are green to look like living plants, while others are brown and crinkly to look like dead leaves or twigs. This puts off most plant-eaters too.

Awesome facts

The peppered moth has speckles on it so it can hide on walls and trees. When pollution makes walls and tree trunks darker, darker peppered moths are more likely to survive.

LEAF INSECT

How many thorn bugs are there on the tree trunk?

19

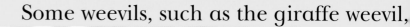

# Crop destroyers

For thousands of years, farmers have fought against insect pests that have tried to eat their crops. Although we now have chemical sprays, greenhouses and special insect-resistant crop breeds, insects still eat vast amounts of our crops every year.

**COLORADO BEETLE**
This little beetle can destroy whole fields of important crops like potatoes and tomatoes.

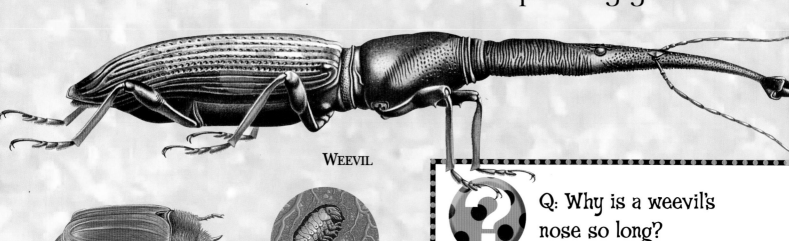

WEEVIL

COCKCHAFER BEETLE    COCKCHAFER GRUB

Cockchafer beetles are serious pests. Their babies, or grubs, live in the soil and nibble away at plant roots. This can destroy entire crops. In 1479, a bishop in Switzerland got so cross with cockchafers that he issued a law banning them from his land!

**Q: Why is a weevil's nose so long?**

A: Weevils are a type of beetle with a long snout. Many weevils feed on crops and on stored food such as grain and rice. They use their long snouts to bore and tunnel their way into their food. The snout has tiny biting jaws at the tip. The weevil's feelers are on the sides of the snout.

have a snout longer than their body!

## Locust life cycles

Locusts lay their eggs in burrows in the ground. When they hatch, the babies can only hop, not fly. As they get older, they start to fly and set off in swarms to look for food. In dry years, they are only a nuisance, but when rain is plentiful, they multiply rapidly and form huge swarms that can destroy crops over vast areas.

LOCUST

SHORT-HORNED GRASSHOPPER

One square kilometre of swarm can have an average of around 75 million locusts.

Some types of grasshopper, including locusts, can travel in swarms up to 160 km wide and 480 km long. These swarms can be so high and dense that they obscure the sun and darken the land. The swarms can strip a field bare in a few minutes.

**21**

HEAD
LICE

Many people have
had 'nits'. Nits are
the eggs of head
lice – tiny bugs
that live in
people's hair.
They have special
claws for holding
onto hairs, and feed
on blood from your
scalp. When a head
louse bites you, it
injects a special
chemical to keep your
blood nice and runny.
This can make your
head very itchy.

Q: How did the deathwatch
beetle get its name?

A: Deathwatch beetles bore tiny
tunnels in wooden furniture. They
live inside the tunnels and make a
tapping noise with their jaws against the
sides. People used to think that when they
heard this noise, it meant that someone in
the house was about to die.

Bedbugs feed on human blood. They
live around, under or in beds, and can
give you a painful bite in the night.
Once a bedbug bites one person, it gets
a taste for their blood and will ignore
everyone else.

BEDBUGS

Silverfish
are not fish,
but silvery, fish-
shaped insects. They like
to live in houses, behind
pictures and in
damp corners.

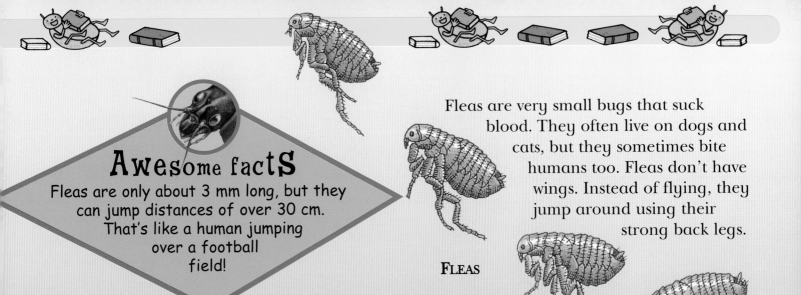

**Awesome facts**

Fleas are only about 3 mm long, but they can jump distances of over 30 cm. That's like a human jumping over a football field!

Fleas are very small bugs that suck blood. They often live on dogs and cats, but they sometimes bite humans too. Fleas don't have wings. Instead of flying, they jump around using their strong back legs.

**FLEAS**

# Horrible house pests

Even if your house is clean and tidy, there are probably quite a few bugs living in it. If it's damp and dirty, there will be millions! Some bugs like dark corners of basements and bathrooms, some feast on the food in your kitchen, and some live on your pets, or even on you.

# Bugs and disease

Some bugs cause serious problems for other living things, including plants, animals and humans. For example, biting insects sometimes carry diseases that get passed on to whoever they bite. Others carry bacteria (germs) on their bodies.

**Awesome facts**
In the 14th century, millions of people died all over Europe from the Black Death, or bubonic plague. It was spread by fleas that lived on rats.

MAGGOTS
Maggots are baby flies.

ADULT FLY

When flies eat, they spit on their food and stamp on it to dissolve it, then suck it up. This leaves lots of germs behind.

Houseflies get everywhere. They lay their eggs on dead animals, animal dung, or rotting food. They feed on sugar in sugar bowls and plates of food left uncovered in the kitchen. They can easily pick up germs and carry them to fresh food as they fly around.

24

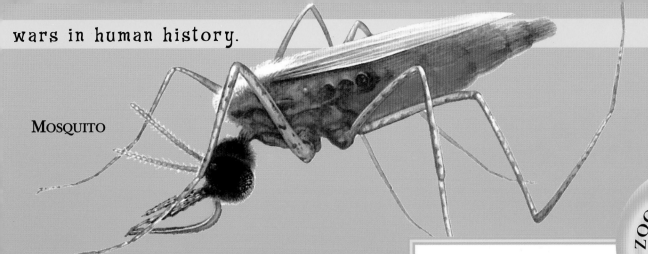

MOSQUITO

Some types of mosquito in hot countries can give you a disease called malaria when they bite you. It gives you a fever, and can be deadly. Another insect, the tsetse fly, spreads a disease called sleeping sickness. Both these diseases kill thousands of people every year.

TSETSE FLY

# Plant disease

The elm bark beetle carries a fungus, a living thing related to mushrooms. When the beetle burrows into an elm tree to feed on it, the fungus gets into the tree and spreads all over it. It makes the leaves wilt, and the tree dies. Millions of elm trees have been wiped out in this way.

zoom in on...

Q: Are maggots really useful in medicine?

A: Yes! Because maggots eat rotting flesh, they are used to keep wounds clean by nibbling away any rotten, infected parts.

There are more than 5,000 species of cockroach. They range from the size of a honeybee to bigger than a computer mouse. Cockroaches can fly, and the biggest ones can have a wingspan of nearly 30 cm.

**TROPICAL COCKROACH**
These brightly coloured cockroaches have cerci. Cerci work like feelers to detect vibrations in the air.

**FALSE DEATH'S-HEAD COCKROACH**
This large cockroach comes from South America. Some people keep them as pets!

Cerci

# Clever cockroaches

Cockroaches look a bit like beetles, but they actually belong to their own special insect family. They are very tough and can survive cold, heat, damp and starvation. Many people think of them as household pests. In fact, although some cockroaches live in people's houses, many more types live in the wild.

26

## How low can they go . . . ?

Most types of cockroach prefer warm places. But they can withstand temperatures as low as 0°C, or freezing, for up to two days. They can also survive being dunked in water, and they can live without food for up to two months.

AMERICAN COCKROACH

Cockroaches are so good at crawling over obstacles, scientists have copied their bodies to make robot insects.

American cockroaches are the largest of the house-infesting cockroach pests. They live behind cupboards and come out at night to feast on crumbs and leftovers.

27

# Recyclers

Many bugs provide a vital service for our planet, by feeding on dead plants and animals, and animal dung. Creatures that do this are called recyclers. If it weren't for them, the Earth would be covered in a deep layer of rotten rubbish.

## Tiny helper

Many recycling animals are tiny. The feather-winged beetle is the world's smallest beetle at just 0.3 mm long – smaller than a full stop. It nibbles the mould that grows on dead plant and animal matter, and breaks it down into chemicals that enrich the soil.

zoom in on...

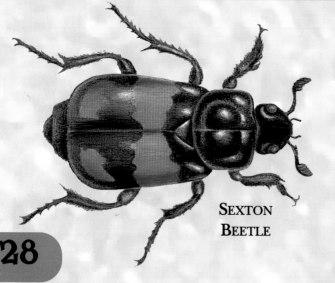

SEXTON BEETLE

A sexton is an old word for a grave digger. The sexton beetle gets its name because it buries dead animals. A male and a female work together to dig under the body of a dead bird or mouse until it sinks into the ground. Then the female lays her eggs on it. When they hatch, the babies feed on the body.

dung beetle. They said he rolled the sun across the sky.

SPRINGTAIL

**SPRINGTAILS**
Springtails live in compost heaps, leaf litter and soil. They help to break down waste into useful chemicals that plants can absorb from the soil. Springtails get their name because they jump around by flicking their tails.

**Q: What do dung beetles do with dung?**

A: Dung beetles collect dung from large animals such as elephants. They can smell dung even before it hits the ground, and start heading towards it. They form it into perfect balls and roll it away into their burrows, where they use it to feed their babies.

# Helpful bugs

Although some bugs are pests, others are very useful to humans. For thousands of years, some types of bug have been helping farmers by eating crop pests. In many parts of the world, humans also use bugs as food.

**LACEWING**
Lacewings and their larvae feed on aphids, which are crop pests. The larvae are sometimes called 'aphid lions'. They cover themselves with plant fibres so that the aphids don't see them coming.

Bugs contain a lot of protein and many people around the world eat them. In Colombia, fried ants are a local delicacy. In Kenya, people eat moth burgers, and in the Australian outback, big fat beetle larvae are considered a tasty snack.

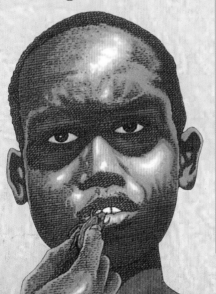

zoom in on...

## Organic gardening

Organic gardening and farming means growing plants without using chemicals to kill pests or weeds. To get rid of aphids and other pests, organic gardeners release killer bugs such as ladybirds into their gardens.

# Glossary

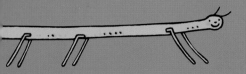
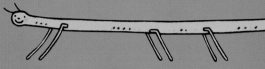

**Abdomen**
One of the three body parts of an insect. All insects have three body parts – a head, a thorax and an abdomen.

**Antennae**
Feelers found on an insect's head. All insects have two antennae.

**Bacteria**
Microscopic living things, some of which can cause disease in animals or plants.

**Camouflage**
The way an animal blends in with its surroundings to escape being noticed by another animal.

**Cerci**
Two 'feelers' on the end of a cockroach's abdomen. They detect vibrations in the air.

**Courtship**
The way that a male and a female animal prepare for mating. They are often trying to impress each other.

**Elytra**
Hard wing cases that cover and protect a beetle's wings.

**Exoskeleton**
The hard covering around the body of an insect that forms a protective armour for its soft, internal organs.

**Fossil**
The remains of any plant or animal, usually preserved in rock.

**Larva**
A young insect. Larvae can look like a small version of the adult, or they can look completely different.

**Metamorphosis**
The striking change some insects go through from larva to adult.

**Nymph**
A name for some types of young insects, such as baby dragonflies.

**Predator**
A flesh-eater – an animal that hunts other animals for food.

**Prey**
An animal that is caught and then eaten by another animal.

**Recycler**
Insects or other living things that break down dead plant and animal matter into chemicals that enrich the soil.

**Species**
The scientific word for a type of living thing. Animals of the same species can breed together.

**Thorax**
One of the three body parts of an insect. See abdomen.

**True bug**
A type of insect. True bugs look a bit like beetles, but instead of jaws they have a sucking mouth shaped like a straw.

31

# Index

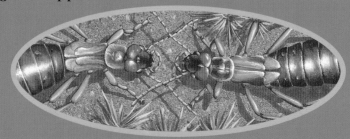